The Challenger Disaster

CORNERSTONES OF FREEDOM™

SECOND SERIES

Tim McNeese

Children's Press®
A Division of Scholastic Inc.
New York • Toronto • London • Auckland • Sydney
Mexico City • New Delhi • Hong Kong
Danbury, Connecticut

Photographs © 2003: AP/Wide World Photos/Steve Helber: 12; Corbis
Images: 8 (James L. Amos), 22 (Bettmann), 30 (Shelley Gazin), 38 (Roger
Ressmeyer); NASA: top cover, bottom cover, 3, 4, 6 bottom, 6 top, 7, 9,
10, 11, 15, 18, 21, 24, 25, 26, 28, 29, 33, 34, 36, 37, 40, 41, 44 right,
44 left, 45 bottom, 45 top, 45 center.

Library of Congress Cataloging-in-Publication Data
McNeese, Tim.
  The Challenger Disaster / Tim McNeese.
      p. cm. — (Cornerstones of freedom. Second series)
  Summary: Recounts events surrounding the explosion of the space shut-
tle Challenger in 1986, the first shuttle to carry a civilian passenger, and
discusses the impact of this disaster on the U.S. space program.
  Includes bibliographical references and index.
    ISBN 0-516-24222-9
    1. Challenger (Spacecraft)—Accidents—Juvenile literature.
2. Space vehicle accidents—United States—Juvenile literature.
[1. Challenger (Spacecraft)—Accidents. 2. Space shuttles—Accidents.]
I. Title. II. Series.
TL867.M365 2003
363.12'465—dc21
                                                    2003005606

1 2 3 4 5 6 7 8 9 10 R 12 11 10 09 08 07 06 05 04 03

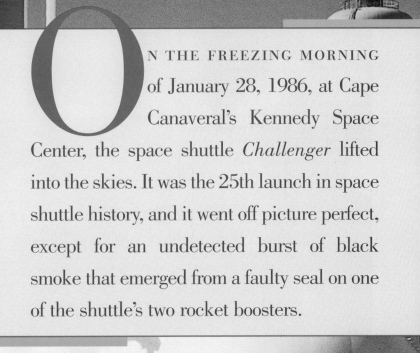

ON THE FREEZING MORNING of January 28, 1986, at Cape Canaveral's Kennedy Space Center, the space shuttle *Challenger* lifted into the skies. It was the 25th launch in space shuttle history, and it went off picture perfect, except for an undetected burst of black smoke that emerged from a faulty seal on one of the shuttle's two rocket boosters.

LIQUIFIED HYDROGEN
FLAMMABLE GAS

HYDROGEN
E GAS

This cloud of smoke actually consists of exhaust from the main engine, a plume from the solid rocket booster, and an expanding ball of gas from the external fuel tank just seconds after *Challenger* exploded in flight.

Onboard was the first civilian passenger, a social studies teacher from New Hampshire. Millions of America's school children sat glued to televisions in schools across the country, inspired by this first "space teacher." But, as *Challenger* STS 51-L rocketed off its launch pad that cold, winter's day, gaining speed and altitude with each passing second, the booster seal cracked open, sending a jet of flame lashing out toward the shuttle's gigantic fuel tank. Within 73 seconds of launch, the *Challenger* and the known future of the American space program exploded into an angry, orange ball of flame and destruction.

A NEW ERA FOR SPACE FLIGHT

The era of the space shuttle began in 1972, just three years after the first Americans walked on the Moon. On April 12, 1981, National Air and Space Agency (NASA) launched the first of its shuttle flights, known as STS-1 (**Space Transportation System**). Blasting off from the Kennedy Space Center, the space shuttle *Columbia* went up with two astronauts onboard on a mission that lasted 54 hours, 22 minutes. In November, a second launch was made. With these two successful shuttle flights, the American space program had turned an important corner.

While spacecraft launched during the 1960s and 1970s featured capsules mounted on the noses of immense rockets, the space shuttle was different. It could be launched more than one time, making it a reusable spaceship. Each

shuttle was designed to be launched into space orbit at least 100 times.

The shuttle resembles a large commercial jetliner with two wings and three great engines called the space shuttle main engines (SSME) located at its tail-end. The entire shuttle measures about the same as a Boeing 727. Just like airplanes, the shuttle has wheels to land on runways, and a cockpit, or **flight deck**, is situated near the front of the shuttle where the pilot controls the space plane. Below the flight deck are the crew quarters where each shuttle team eats, sleeps, and generally lives. Space shuttles are designed to carry crews of between two and seven astronauts

A space shuttle launch at the Kennedy Space Center. Although the shuttle is designed to return to Earth and land on its own, it is carried from Earth by a booster rocket.

Challenger makes a successful landing at Edwards Air Force base. The space shuttle is the first vehicle capable of traveling beyond Earth's atmosphere in outer space and returning to land on Earth so that it can make another flight.

for missions typically lasting between a week and ten days, sometimes even two weeks.

Between the cockpit and the engines is a lengthy **bay**, a compartment where special cargo, such as satellites, can ride to delivery in space. The bay is large enough to easily accommodate a passenger bus. Two long doors cover the bay and open to release satellites or provide storage space for retrieved spacecraft.

A LITTLE BOOST FOR LAUNCHING

While the space shuttle lands horizontally like an airplane, it is launched into space vertically from a launch site. This means the spacecraft must push itself straight up off the **launch pad**. This requires three powerful engines. The engines mounted on a shuttle are massive. They are large enough to produce enough **thrust**, or energy to cause **lift**, off the launch pad. Among the largest vehicle engines on Earth, they burn fuel at a rate of 45,000 gallons (171,000 liters) per minute! This is an amount equal to an average-sized backyard swimming pool. Since this quantity is enormous, the shuttle is not large enough to carry all the fuel it needs to rocket into space,

A marvelous work of human ingenuity is reduced to scraps of metal as *Challenger* is blown to pieces.

7

This view of workers inside the space shuttle's external fuel tank provides some indication of the vessel's size. The external fuel tank is made of aluminum.

complete a weeklong mission, and return to Earth. So, the shuttle needs some extra help getting off the ground.

Before launch, the shuttle is attached to a gigantic, 150-foot long, external fuel tank. This huge, rust-orange-colored tank holds more than half a million gallons (2 million liters) of solid fuel. This fuel is a mixture of **liquid oxygen** (about 27 percent)

The shuttle's external fuel tank falls to Earth after being jettisoned by the shuttle's crew. The release of the external fuel tank usually completes the launch portion of a space shuttle mission.

A HALF TON OF PAINT

In 1981, when the shuttle program began, the huge fuel tank was painted white to match the white shuttle orbiter and the matching twin rocket boosters. However, this extra coat of white paint was discontinued by the year's end. Engineers calculated that the extra paint added an unnecessary 1,000 pounds of weight to the tank. Since then, the fuel tank has retained its red oxide primer color.

and **liquid hydrogen** (about 73 percent). The tank provides all the fuel required for **lift-off** from a launch pad and to achieve enough altitude to go into **orbit**. But the tank is so large and heavy, the shuttle engines cannot possibly launch both the orbiter and the fuel tank.

A third element must be added to the launch site before a shuttle can be fired into the heavens. A pair of matching **solid-fuel rocket boosters** (SRBs) is fitted between the shuttle and the fuel tank, each beneath one of the wings of the space plane. These boosters provide enough lift to

The space shuttle awaits take-off. The tragic disasters that befell *Challenger* and, more recently, *Columbia* have led many people to question the value of human space flight.

launch themselves, the orbiter, and the fuel tank. The combined weight of these pieces of space equipment, plus all the required fuel, is nearly 4.4 million pounds (approximately 2 million kilograms). This means the boosters must provide enough thrust to not only lift it all off the ground, but rocket the whole combination of space parts into space.

Within a few years of the first launch, NASA built a small fleet of shuttle orbiters. *Enterprise* was a test vehicle and never flew in space. *Columbia* flew the first five shuttle space missions during 1981 and 1982. *Challenger* joined the space fleet in 1983, then a fourth, *Discovery*, came on line the following year. *Atlantis* was introduced in 1985.

During those years, *Challenger* was launched more than any other shuttle and achieved several "firsts" for shuttle flights, including the first shuttle launch at night (STS-8), shuttle space walk (STS-6), and the first shuttle to capture and repair a satellite in space. *Challenger* also launched the first woman (STS-7) and first African American (STS-8) of the U.S. space program.

When the space shuttle program was first created on paper, it was assumed the reusable spacecraft would fly to and from a planned orbiting space station. However, when Congress cut that program for financial reasons, the shuttles were primarily used to transport satellites into space and retrieve malfunctioning satellites for repair. Also, shuttle crews used the orbiter for experiments in space, the kinds that would have been performed on a space station.

The January 28th launch of the space shuttle *Challenger* was NASA's second for the year. NASA was looking to achieve new heights of success in

SHIPS OF ANOTHER SORT

The first four shuttles constructed for space flight—*Columbia*, *Challenger*, *Discovery*, and *Atlantis*—were named after sailing ships famous for exploration. *Columbia* was an 1830s U.S. Naval frigate that sailed around the world. Another Navy sailing vessel, *Challenger*, explored the Atlantic and Pacific Oceans between 1872 and 1876. *Discovery* was named for two ships, including Henry Hudson's 1610 vessel and one commanded by Captain Cook. *Atlantis* was an oceanographic vessel that sailed more than 500,000 miles between 1930 and 1966. *Enterprise* was named for the fictional starship on the 1960s TV series, *Star Trek*.

The Hubble Space Telescope (HST) resumes its mission of observing the universe after being repaired by astronauts in the space shuttle. The space shuttle was used to release and repair HST on several occasions.

space. The agency's fleet of four shuttles was fully operational and all four had made at least two successful trips into space since 1981. Fifteen shuttle trips were already being planned. One was to launch the largest telescope for space use, the

After lift-off had been delayed by a day, *Challenger*'s crew was all smiles as they made their way to the launch pad on the morning of January 28, 1986. From the front, the crew was payload specialist Greg Jarvis, mission specialist Ellison S. Onizuka, school teacher Christa McAuliffe, and pilot Mike Smith.

Hubble. New communications satellites were to be launched for orbit. Several probes bound for the distant planet Jupiter were also being prepared.

THE CREW OF THE CHALLENGER

As NASA assembled the seven-person crew for the tenth scheduled *Challenger* mission, dubbed STS 51-L, the space agency brought together a unique group. Five crew members were government employees, including two former Air Force officers and one U.S. Navy pilot. While three of the crew members were white men, a fourth was Japanese American and the fifth crewman was African American. Two crew members were women; one of them was Jewish. Each brought his or her own unique talents and skills to contribute to the planned *Challenger* mission.

A former Air Force pilot, Francis R. "Dick" Scobee, was selected as the mission's commander. The pilot for 51-L was U.S. Naval Commander Michael J. Smith. In addition to the flight commander and its pilot, the *Challenger* crew included three mission specialists. Dr. Judith A. Resnik was one of the first woman astronauts accepted by NASA. Another of *Challenger*'s mission specialists was Dr. Ronald E. McNair. The third mission specialist for space shuttle mission 51-L was a Japanese American named Ellison S. Onizuka. Onizuka

SHUTTLE FLIGHTS BY NUMBER

The flight number of *Challenger*'s last mission was 51-L. But what did the number mean? NASA identified its first nine shuttle missions simply as STS-1, STS-2, and so on. (STS is short for Space Transportation System). Beginning with the 10th shuttle flight, each number or letter held a special meaning. The '5' indicated the fiscal year (1985-86) when the shuttle's flight was originally scheduled. The '1' indicated the launch site, Kennedy Space Center. (A '2' meant Vandenburg Air Force Base in California.) The 'L' (the 12th letter of the alphabet) stood for the flight order for that fiscal year, the 12th planned launch.

had flown on one previous shuttle mission, *Discovery* STS-51-C. Gregory B. Jarvis earned a seat on *Challenger* 51-L as a payload specialist.

A TEACHER IN SPACE

The seventh crew member selected for *Challenger* 51-L was a school teacher from Concord, New Hampshire. How Sharon Christa McAuliffe came to be part of the shuttle crew is a curious story.

For two decades, all American spacecraft flights had been made only by highly trained American astronauts. Starting in the early 1980s, the shuttle crews became increasingly multicultural. In 1983, the first European astronaut flew on the shuttle *Columbia*. Other non-Americans followed, including a Canadian, additional Europeans, and a Mexican. Such passengers were logical for shuttle flights, since the planned space station was intended to have an international crew.

By 1985, crew members included those with no actual space training. In April, a United States senator, Jake Garn, flew on *Discovery*'s 51-D mission. Two months later, a Saudi Arabian prince became a member of the *Discovery* crew. Then, Congressman Bill Nelson requested a shuttle ride. That flight took place just two weeks before the launch of *Challenger* 51-L. While such passengers were allowed to join shuttle missions for political reasons, some astronauts did not like the practice. Every time a non-astronaut was allowed to fly on a shuttle, a highly trained astronaut had to give up his seat.

Christa McAuliffe crouches on a seat at *Challenger*'s control panel. A social studies teacher in Concord, New Hampshire, McAuliffe was chosen by NASA to be the first civilian in space. NASA hoped that the participation of civilians would increase public awareness and support of the space program.

In August 1984, President Ronald Reagan announced the first "citizen passenger" onboard a shuttle flight was to be a teacher. NASA saw the "Teacher in Space" mission as a unique opportunity to generate a new level of public interest in the shuttle program and space in general. Shuttle flights had become so routine to the public, many people hardly paid any attention to them. With a school teacher onboard, millions would watch STS 51-L.

More than 11,000 teachers applied for the opportunity to ride on the shuttle, and after an involved application

THE RELUCTANT ASTRONAUT

Although Utah senator Jake Garn was not a professionally-trained astronaut, he came to his shuttle mission with experience flying military aircraft. However, he did not do well in space. Sent onboard *Discovery* in April 1985, Garn became so spacesick the crew renamed the orbiter "The Vomit Comet."

process, the Concord High School social studies teacher was picked. On her application, McAuliffe had written "Space is a unique opportunity to fulfill my early fantasies. I watched the space program being born and would like to participate." Once selected, she took a leave from teaching while NASA paid her salary and put her through astronaut training. On July 19, 1985, the 37-year-old McAuliffe was chosen to fly on a future *Challenger* mission.

Since a civilian was onboard, NASA wanted everything to go without a hitch, especially since McAuliffe's involvement would generate a higher level of interest in the mission than usual. The Concord school teacher became a student, as she read books and training materials to give her a clearer understanding of what being an astronaut is all about. She experienced the high-tech training machines designed to help her become accustomed to the pressures and rigors of space. Some of NASA's astronauts were skeptical of non-professionals flying in space. Astronaut Judith Resnik had once confided to a friend, "What are we going to do with these people?" Yet McAuliffe intended to bring the same level of professionalism to the space program that she brought to her classroom at Concord High School. In an interview, the excited teacher said "Imagine me teaching from space, all over the world, touching so many people's lives. That's a teacher's dream!"

THE MISSION OF CHALLENGER 51-L

Challenger 51-L was planned as a six-day, 34-minute mission. Along with the routine delivery of satellites into space and scientific experiments to be conducted, McAuliffe was to teach a live telecast of a school lesson to children across the country. Finally, the mission would retrieve one of the delivered satellites before returning to Earth.

DELAYS AND OTHER PROBLEMS

The *Challenger* mission was originally scheduled to launch in December, 1985. But equipment problems and weather conditions, including high winds, caused the mission launch date to be moved back by several weeks. The launch date was reset for January 22. Several other launch dates came and went. With the launch finally scheduled for January 26, both the weather and a stuck side hatch pushed the date back again, first to January 27, then to Tuesday, January 28.

On the morning of January 28, 1986, the skies above the Kennedy Space Center were clear, just right for a space launch. However, morning temperatures were well below freezing, down in the low twenties. As they inspected the launch site, NASA personnel, including an "ice-team," discovered hundreds of heavy icicles hanging from the **Fixed Service Structure**, which served as the support for the vertically positioned space shuttle. Some of the ice formations were 16 inches long. The **gantry**, or

Parts of *Challenger* are clearly visible in this picture taken just seconds after the explosion that claimed the life of each member of the crew.

walkway, and the handrails the astronauts were to use to reach their spacecraft were sheathed in ice, too. The ice and cold temperatures were an important factor in the decision by mission engineers and scientists to launch *Challenger* that morning.

The company that built the two solid-fuel rocket boosters, Morton Thiokol, had employees at the space center that morning. These experts knew better than anyone how the boosters worked. Their earlier studies had led them to recommend that the SRBs should not be launched if the temperature was below 53 degrees Fahrenheit. After consulting, the Morton Thiokol engineers recommended the shuttle launch be delayed. However, NASA managers did not want to hear the negative suggestion. One NASA project manager criticized the suggestion not to launch, saying if it didn't happen then "we won't be able to launch until April." Despite the suggestions not to launch, NASA officials gave the shuttle the green light to go.

AN ILL-FATED LAUNCH

At 11:38 A.M., after several hours delay, the solid-fuel rocket boosters burst into action with a thunderous roar. The giant fuel tank and twin booster rockets spewed hot flames and gases, as the SRBs burned ten tons of fuel a second. Slowly, the space shuttle *Challenger* rose from Launch Pad 39B. As the shuttle separated from its moorings, the spacecraft's computers began their work of putting the ship and crew into space. Thousands of spectators watched near the launch site, with high hopes for the crew.

Among the joyous crowd were the parents and sister of teacher Christa McAuliffe.

Rocketing skyward, the crew inside *Challenger* felt their space shuttle turning, placing them upside-down, according to plan. They began experiencing the weight of great G-force, pressure placed on the body by gravity and acceleration. As the shuttle, fuel tank, and SRBs worked in unison, the crew began to feel the effects of an expected acceleration to 17,000 miles per hour.

During the following 73 seconds, nothing seemed amiss, and the crew proceeded through the routine instrument checks. *Challenger's* operational recorder voice tape recorded the comments of Scobee, Smith, Onizuka, and Resnik, as they went about their duties as trained professionals. Other than a comment by *Challenger* pilot Mike Smith concerning strong winds, there was no concern, anxiousness, or fear among the crew members concerning what might happen next.

When the shuttle reached 19,000 feet, it achieved **Mach 1**, a speed equal to the speed of sound. Pilot Smith throttled the ship's engines back, expecting a "boom" caused by breaking the sound barrier. During the following 14 seconds, strong, high altitude winds buffeted the spacecraft intensely. But *Challenger* finally broke through the disturbances, as Smith throttled up the boosters. Just one minute and 10 seconds after lift-off, *Challenger* 51-L, the 25th shuttle launch in American history, reached an altitude of 50,000 feet— nearly 10 miles up. Only then did the entire crew begin to

* * * *

Challenger exploded 73 seconds into its last flight. In the technical language of NASA engineers, the catastrophe was a category of event abbreviated as LOV, which stands for "loss of vehicle."

relax. At T-1:10, the shuttle's voice recorder taped Commander Scobee saying: "Roger, go at throttle up." Three seconds later, Pilot Smith spoke the last recorded words from anyone onboard STS 51-L: "Uh-oh."

Onlookers gaze in horror at the fiery demise of *Challenger.*

THE DESTRUCTION OF CHALLENGER

At that moment, a thunderous explosion rocked the spacecraft and its crew. A tiny fire had been burning since lift-off, but had gone undetected. It was centered in a weakened ring connection on the right booster rocket, where high winds had stretched open the unstable seal in the SRB. This caused a super-heated stream of flame to burn a hole in the shuttle's fuel tank, igniting *Challenger*'s fuel supply of 300,000 gallons of liquid hydrogen and 100,000 gallons of oxygen, which turned both mixtures into a gigantic, flying bomb. The unearthly blast ripped *Challenger* to pieces. Released from their moorings, the two SRBs continued to burn, careening off in two directions. A writer for *Time* magazine later described the view as "a giant monster in the sky, its two claws reaching frantically forward."

From the ground, the anxious crowd of shuttle watchers sitting in a special viewing stand felt their excitement turn to shocked disbelief. The *Challenger* explosion was visible from the ground, and Christa McAuliffe's parents and sister watched in tormented horror as the sky filled with several long streams of thick white smoke. The three family members clung to one another as the tragedy unfolded before their eyes. Some in the crowd watched and hoped that *Challenger* would fly out of the fiery disaster and survive intact. But this was impossible.

THE FATE OF THE CREW

As the solid-fuel rocket boosters (SRBs) exploded, the space orbiter disintegrated. Yet the crew compartment, located on the opposite end of the spacecraft, away from the source of the explosion, remained in one piece. The shuttle cabin continued to climb in the skies above the Atlantic for several seconds, reaching an altitude of approximately 65,000 feet. Then, the compartment, containing all seven crew members, began to drop to Earth. The free-falling shuttle cabin hurtled toward the ocean for a distance of 12 miles and did not hit the waters of the Atlantic Ocean for nearly three minutes.

Was the crew still alive? What went on in the crew compartment following the fiery explosion that destroyed their space shuttle? Was there anything they could do to save themselves? Not all these questions can be answered with certainty. According to the government report of the tragedy, issued five months later, experts stated that when the crew cabin was recovered from the Atlantic, all seven were still strapped into their seats. The report indicated that the explosion that tore the shuttle apart was probably not close enough to the crew to cause their deaths or even break the shuttle compartment's windows. The report also revealed that crew members, following the explosion, had activated three of the four onboard air-supply canisters, indicating someone, at least, was still alive after the fiery blast.

But how did the crew members actually die? Did they live through their horrific descent back to Earth? The findings of the experts suggest that the crew might have become unconscious sometime after the explosion, but "not certainly." Also, the descent itself would not have caused enough gravitational force to "cause death or serious injury." The seven-member crew of the space shuttle

A DELAYED RECOVERY

When *Challenger* exploded in the morning sky of January 28, U.S. Navy and coast guard vessels, including ships and submarines, were immediately dispatched to the waters where the shuttle debris fell. Navy divers eventually recovered approximately 35 percent of the *Challenger* orbiter, plus half of the pieces of both the SRBs and the fuel tank. Although divers searched desperately for the key piece of the shuttle—the crew compartment—it was not found until six weeks after the accident.

Wreckage of *Challenger* is loaded aboard the coast guard vessel *Dallas*. A flotilla of navy and coast guard vessels was deployed across a broad area of the Atlantic Ocean off the Florida coast to recover such wreckage.

This section of *Challenger*'s right wing was recovered by a navy rescue and salvage ship in 70 feet of water about 12 nautical miles northeast of the Kennedy Space Center, the shuttle's launch site in Florida.

Challenger 51-L mission may have survived the destruction of their ship and remained conscious and unhurt during their two-minute and forty-five second plunge to Earth. However, the impact of the crew compartment with the ocean's surface probably caused their deaths. Experts estimate the cabin struck the water at a speed of 207 miles per hour.

During the hours following *Challenger*'s explosion, burning pieces of the spacecraft, its boosters, and the fuel tank rained down to Earth, drifting into the quiet, blue waters of the Atlantic Ocean.

IN THE AFTERMATH OF LOSS

The American public was shocked and dismayed at the destruction of the space shuttle *Challenger*. Many Americans had paid special attention to the launch of *Challenger* 51-L because of Christa McAuliffe. Millions of people watched the launch of the shuttle that Monday morning on television. Vice President George H. W. Bush flew to the Kennedy Space Center to meet with family members of the lost crew and offer the nation's best wishes.

President Reagan, who was scheduled to deliver his annual State of the Union message, cancelled his speech. Instead, he made a televised address to the American

An underwater camera captured fish swimming by a submerged solid rocket booster from *Challenger*. The booster was found about 210 feet below the surface of the Atlantic Ocean, approximately 23 miles east of the Kennedy Space Center.

26

people that afternoon. From the Oval Office, Reagan tried to comfort the families of the crew and encourage the spirit of all Americans. Of the crew, the president said, "They wished to serve and they did—they served us all." Aware that many of those who had watched the launch and the fiery explosion that morning were children in school, Reagan assured them: "I know it's hard to understand that sometimes painful things like this happen. It's all part of the process of exploration and discovery; it's all part of taking a chance and expanding man's horizons."

During the previous twenty years, NASA had launched humans into space 55 times and returned them all safely. One former U.S. astronaut, John Glenn from Ohio, stated what should have been obvious to everyone: "We always knew there would be a day like this. We're dealing with speeds and powers and complexities we've never dealt with before."

EXPLAINING THE DISASTER'S CAUSES

Following the disaster, President Reagan called for an investigation to determine the cause of the explosion. All planned space shuttle launches were cancelled for the immediate future.

When the panel of experts—including astronauts, engineers and respected scientists—concluded their investigations, they issued a detailed report summarizing their findings in June 1986, after months of examining the evidence, conducting interviews, and reviewing past shuttle flights. Perhaps the most important portion of the

This storage facility was used to hold recovered pieces of *Challenger* after it exploded. There, engineers and technicians worked to piece together the wreckage in an attempt to discover the cause of the disaster.

report addressed the obvious question: What caused the explosion that destroyed *Challenger* on that cold, fateful morning in January? Several factors were highlighted for blame, including equipment failures, weather conditions, and poor decision-making.

The question of equipment failure received much study. The space shuttles flown by the United States are among the most complicated machines in the world, consisting of tens of thousands of parts involving hundreds of systems. Although *Challenger* itself did not malfunction that tragic morning, one of its solid-fuel rocket boosters did.

Unknown to NASA engineers and launch personnel, just as *Challenger* began its lift-off, a synthetic rubber joint seal, called an **O-ring**, developed a leak. The rings seal the joints of the SRBs. The launch site camera that would have

Technicians at the Vehicle Assembly Building examine how the space shuttle's rocket boosters have been sealed into place before launching. The investigation into the *Challenger* disaster would focus on such seals.

A REVEALING DEMONSTRATION

One of the main problems with the O-rings used to seal the joints of *Challenger*'s twin rocket boosters was how they reacted to cold temperatures. Launch temperature had been 36 degrees F, 17 degrees colder than the O-ring manufacturer recommended for the rubbery seals. During the investigation, a member of the study commission, Dr. Richard Feynman, made a public demonstration showing how vulnerable the O-rings were to the cold. He dropped a piece of the O-ring rubber into a glass of ice water, then took it out and snapped the hardened material in two.

Physicist Dr. Richard Feynman holds an O-ring. One of the world's most brilliant scientists, Feynman was instrumental in determining that it was the failure of this simple part that brought about the catastrophic destruction of *Challenger*.

revealed this problem was not working the morning of the launch. The flawed seal did not cause an immediate problem for the shuttle. But 59 seconds into its flight, the internal pressure on the right-hand SRB caused the O-ring leak to expand, sending out a jet of flame which, seconds later, ignited the large fuel tank. It is extremely likely that the high winds *Challenger* experienced only heightened the problem, causing the O-ring joint to fail.

While NASA officials did not know of the particular O-ring leak before the launch, they were aware of the limits of these rubber-like connectors. The morning of the pre-launch, engineers of the company that manufactured the O-rings, Morton Thiokol, had advised against the launch. The below-normal temperatures had probably rendered the O-rings hard and brittle, setting up *Challenger* for a major disaster.

To add to the scope of the design flaw, the investigating commission reported that O-ring damage had occurred during at least 14 of the previous 24 shuttle fleet missions! When it issued its report, the commission suggested several design changes for future SRBs, including the joint seals. The group also proposed a crew escape system be developed to aid launch emergency evacuation.

Why did NASA decide to launch *Challenger* on the morning of January 28, despite warnings by experts against it? The investigation team observed how communication problems within NASA's management had led to the disaster. The report noted "there was a serious flaw in the decision making process leading up to the launch of flight 51-L."

WHAT NASA OFFICIALS KNEW

The 12-member commission that investigated the *Challenger* disaster revealed much information about the disaster that was previously unknown to the public. Perhaps most disappointing was the fact that some NASA officials were aware of the O-ring problem before the loss of *Challenger*. The problem had been considered so serious that the booster rockets had been redesigned without O-rings. NASA had placed the order for the new boosters before the *Challenger* explosion, but they had not yet been completed.

Several reasons may have played a part in the misguided decision. NASA officials felt pressure to launch since the *Challenger* mission date had been set back four times already. Then, there was the teacher, Christa McAuliffe. The mission called for her to teach a lesson in space on Friday, Day Four, of the mission. Another day's delay in launching would have ruined that plan. Years after the *Challenger* disaster, McAuliffe's mother, Grace Corrigan, said she spoke with her daughter the day of the launch. Christa told her NASA had decided to launch on the 28th, and nothing would change that decision. "The word was out that today was the day," said Christa. "Definitely."

AMERICA'S SPACE PROGRAM ON HOLD

Following the *Challenger* disaster, President Reagan told a sorrowful American public: "Sometimes when we reach for the stars, we fall short. But we must press on despite the pain." However, for the moment, the American space program ground to a halt. For two years, no shuttle missions were even scheduled. The head of NASA was replaced by a former astronaut, Admiral Richard Truly. Another dozen NASA officials and Morton Thiokol administrators also resigned by the end of 1986. The space program suffered

The space shuttle, in this instance the ship *Endeavor*, approaches the International Space Station (ISS). The photograph was taken by a member of the crew aboard the ISS.

An astronaut holds on to the arm of the space shuttle's remote manipulator system, or RMS. The RMS allows the shuttle's crew to carry out what NASA calls EVA, or extravehicular activity, such as making repairs to the **Hubble Space Telescope** and other vehicles.

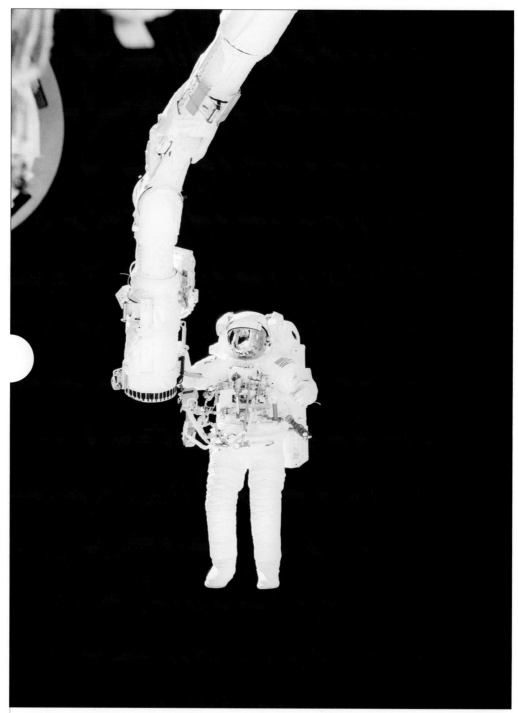

dramatic losses in morale as ten astronauts, with no expectations of being launched into space, quit the program and took other jobs. Truly worked hard to fix NASA's problems, including overseeing the redesign of a new shuttle orbiter. Looking to the future, the space agency director stated: "The NASA can-do spirit is intact. We are going to get back on the track of exploring . . . space."

To recover from the tragic accident, NASA had to rethink its approach to space flight. The process was expensive. Shuttle system repairs and alterations took nearly three years to complete, at a cost of $2.4 billion. The remaining shuttles—*Discovery*, *Columbia*, and *Atlantis*—were remodeled and re-systematized. Among the changes was a completely remodeled solid-fuel rocket booster. They were also built into a new shuttle, *Endeavor*, which finally replaced *Challenger* in 1991. Changes to the shuttle fleet included new safety features, including an emergency escape hatch. Additional upgrades and safety changes continued into the 21st century.

NASA AFTER CHALLENGER

Despite the *Challenger* tragedy, the American space program did recover. Finally, two years after the disaster, NASA scheduled another shuttle mission for *Discovery* for February 1988. But as the date approached, cautious engineers and space personnel, having learned a lesson from the worst disaster in space history, postponed the launch until September 29. When *Discovery* finally blasted off the launch site that fall day, 32 months after *Challenger*, many

Anchored to the arm of the shuttle RMS, this astronaut is positioning a solar array panel during an EVA. Such arrays are used to convert sunlight into electricity by what is known as the photoelectric effect.

Americans felt relieved, hopeful the *Challenger* disaster would never be repeated.

Shuttle flights began to occur with regularity and meet new challenges in space. However, on February 1, 2003, tragedy struck again when the space shuttle *Columbia* STS-107 broke apart after re-entering the Earth's atmosphere. It

Earth's horizon is visible beyond the cargo bay of the space shuttle during a mission flown by *Columbia*, which in 2003 met a similar fate to that of *Challenger*.

An astronaut carries out an EVA aboard the shuttle against the shimmering backdrop of Earth, thousands of miles below.

had completed its sixteen-day mission, solely devoted to scientific research, and was minutes away from landing at Kennedy Space Center in Florida. Again, a brave, seven-member crew was lost, including the first Israeli astronaut to fly in space. The events following this most recent tragedy resembled that of the *Challenger* disaster. A memorial service was held at the Johnson Space Center in Houston, Texas. This time, President George W. Bush offered words of comfort to the families of the crew members and to mourners everywhere.

Following the president's speech, four T-38 jets flew across the sky in tribute to the seven crew members. The planes flew in a symbolic formation, called "Missing Man."

President Ronald Reagan's words, spoken just hours after *Challenger* flew its final, fateful mission in 1986, were appropriate on February 1, 2003: "We will never forget them nor the last time we saw them . . . as they prepared for their journey and waved goodbye and 'slipped the surly bonds of earth to touch the face of God.'"

Powered by the immense thrust of its rocket boosters, the space shuttle leaves the launching pad.

Glossary

bay—a compartment where special cargo, such as satellites, can ride to delivery onboard a space shuttle

Fixed Service Structure—the permanent supports on a launch pad that hold a vertically-positioned space shuttle in place before launch

flight deck—similar to the cockpit of an airplane, it is an instrument center where a pilot flies a space shuttle

G-force—the pressure gravity and acceleration place on a body

gantry—the walkway on the Fixed Service Structure used by astronauts to board the shuttle on the launch pad

launch pad—NASA facility from which a shuttle is delivered into space

lift—the power or force required to raise an object

lift-off—the instant at which a rocket or other craft begins its flight

liquid hydrogen—highly flammable gas maintained in liquid form and used to produce rocket fuel

liquid oxygen—one of two liquid chemicals used in rocket propellants, combined with liquid hydrogen to provide fuel for the space shuttle

Mach 1—a speed equal to the speed of sound

O-rings—the rubbery seals used to connect sections of the solid-fuel rocket boosters to one another

orbit—the path of an object as it revolves around another body

remote manipulator system—a mechanical robotic arm used to deliver and retrieve satellites from the shuttle's cargo bay during flight

solid-fuel rocket boosters (SRBs)—the pair of matching launchers fitted between the shuttle and the fuel tank that provide additional lift for the shuttle during launch

Space Transportation System (STS)—NASA's official name for the space shuttle

thrust—the energy required to cause lift

Timeline: The Challenger

1972

President Richard Nixon gives approval for the development of the space shuttle program.

1981

NASA launches the first of its shuttle flights from Kennedy Space Center. The space shuttle *Columbia* completes a 54 hour, 22 minute mission with two astronauts onboard, John Young and Robert Crippen.

1983

APRIL 4
Challenger becomes NASA's third space shuttle. During its first mission (STS-6) its crew performs the first shuttle space walk.

• • • • • • • • •

JUNE 18
Challenger mission STS-7 includes the first American woman as a member of the astronaut crew.

AUGUST 30
Challenger mission STS-8 involves the first night launch of a shuttle and the first African-American crew member.

1984

Discovery joins the NASA fleet of shuttles.

• • • • • • • • •

August: President Ronald Reagan announced the first "citizen passenger" onboard a shuttle flight will be a teacher.

Disaster

APRIL 12
United States Senator Jake Garn flies as a member of the crew on *Discovery's* 51-D mission.

JULY 19
Social studies teacher Christa McAuliffe is chosen to fly on a future *Challenger* mission. Space shuttle *Atlantis* is added to NASA's fleet of shuttles. Space shuttle *Challenger* is launched into space three times this year.

JANUARY 12
House Congressman Bill Nelson flies on *Columbia* mission STS 61-C.

JANUARY 28
Launch date for *Challenger* STS 51-L. Shuttle launch takes place at 11:38 A.M. (EST). Seventy-three seconds following launch, one of the solid-fuel rocket boosters ignites the fuel tank,

exploding *Challenger*, and killing its seven-person crew. That afternoon, President Reagan addresses the American people to express his sorrow over the loss of the shuttle crew.

JUNE
President's investigating commission issues report on the causes of the *Challenger* explosion. The commission targets poor communication and decision-making within NASA, a faulty O-ring seal, and strong winds as factors leading to the accident.

SEPTEMBER 29
NASA launches the space shuttle *Discovery*, making it the first shuttle launch since the *Challenger* explosion.

To Find Out More

BOOKS

Bergin, Mark and David Salariya. *Space Shuttle*. New York: Scholastic, 1999.

Bredeson, Carmen. *The Challenger Disaster: Tragic Space Flight*. Berkeley Heights, NJ: Enslow Publishers, Inc., 1999.

Lassieur, Allison. *The Space Shuttle*. Danbury, CT: Children's Press, 2000.

Lieurance, Suzanne. *The Space Shuttle Challenger Disaster in American History*. Berkeley Heights, NJ: Enslow Publishers, Inc., 2001.

Spangenburg, Ray and Kit Moser. *Onboard the Space Shuttle*. Danbury, CT: Grolier Publishing, 2002.

ONLINE SITES

www.nasa.gov/kids.html
(Part of the official website for NASA designed for kids)

www.nasa.gov/hqpao/library.html
(Part of the official government website for NASA containing photos, video clips, and sounds)

www-pao.ksc.nasa.gov/chron/sts51-l.html
(Part of the Kennedy Space Center website, which presents information about the *Challenger* Mission 51-L)

Index

About the Author

Tim McNeese is an Associate Professor of History at York College in Nebraska. He has written more than fifty books on everything from the Giza Pyramids to the New York City subway system. He grew up in the Missouri Ozarks, where he remembers watching early space launches on a black-and-white television with his classmates in the school cafeteria. He was in a classroom teaching when he first heard the *Challenger* had exploded. Professor McNeese graduated from York College with his Associate of Arts degree, as well as from Harding University, where he received his Bachelor of Arts degree in history and political science. He received his Master of Arts degree in history from Southwest Missouri State University. Professor McNeese is married to Beverly McNeese, who teaches English at York College.